Coasts

Louise and Richard Spilsbury

www.heinemann.co.uk/library
Visit our website to find out more information about **Heinemann Library** books.

To order:
☎ Phone 44 (0) 1865 888066
▤ Send a fax to 44 (0) 1865 314091
▯ Visit the Heinemann Bookshop at www.heinemann.co.uk/library to browse our catalogue and order online.

First published in Great Britain by Heinemann Library, Halley Court, Jordan Hill, Oxford OX2 8EJ, part of Harcourt Education.

Heinemann is a registered trademark of Harcourt Education Ltd.

Editorial: Lucy Thunder and Helen Cannons
Design: David Poole and Kamae Design
Picture Research: Hannah Taylor and Liz Savery
Production: Edward Moore

Originated by P.T. Repro Multi-Warna
Printed in China by WKT Company Limited

The paper used to print this book comes from sustainable resources.

ISBN 0 431 12120 6
08 07 06 05 04
10 9 8 7 6 5 4 3 2 1

British Library Cataloguing in Publication Data
Spilsbury, Louise and Spilsbury, Richard
Coasts. – (Wild habitats of the British Isles)
577.5′1′0941
A full catalogue record for this book is available from the British Library.

Acknowledgements
The Publishers would like to thank the following for permission to reproduce photographs: FLPA/M Nimmo p**5**; FLPA/Tony Wharton pp**20** bottom, **23**; Heather Angel/Natural Visions p**18**; Jason Hawkes Aerial Photography Library p**4**; Jo Pitson pp**7** bottom, **17**, **21**; Nature Picture Library/Martin H Smith p**7** top; Nature Picture Library/Niall Benvie p**6**; Nature Picture Library/Tim Edwards p**9**; NHPA/David Woodfall pp**10**, **27**; NHPA/Laurie Campbell p**11**; Ordnance Survey pp**14** top, **20** top; OSF/Peter Clarke/SAL p**29**; Oxford Scientific Films/David Fox p**22**; Oxford Scientific Films/Gary & Terry Andrewartha/SAL p**15**; Oxford Scientific Films/Kenneth Day p**12**; Oxford Scientific Films/Paul Kay p**25**; Photofusion/David Hoffman p**28**; Positive Design Consultants/Strangford Lough Management Advisory Committee p**24**; Woodfall Wild Images pp**13**, **16**; Woodfall Wild Images/David Woodfall pp**14** bottom, **24** bottom; Woodfall Wild Images/Jeremy Moore p**26**; Woodfall Wild Images/Sue Scott p**8**.

Cover photograph of a rocky coastline, reproduced with permission of NHPA/G J Cambridge.

The Publishers would like to thank Michael Scott, wildlife consultant and writer, for his assistance in the preparation of this book.

Every effort has been made to contact copyright holders of any material reproduced in this book. Any omissions will be rectified in subsequent printings if notice is given to the Publishers.

Contents

Any words appearing in the text in bold, **like this**, are explained in the Glossary.

Coastal habitats

A coast is the edge of the land where it meets the sea or ocean. The British Isles are made up of two large and many smaller islands, so they are surrounded by coastline. Coasts are dynamic places – that means they are always changing. They change every day as the water flows in and out with the **tides**. Coasts also change shape slowly, over many weeks and years, as the action of the waves, wind and rain work on them.

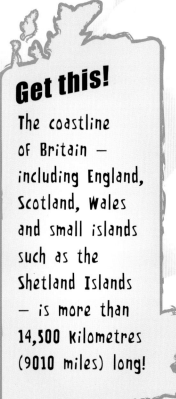

Get this!

The coastline of Britain – including England, Scotland, Wales and small islands such as the Shetland Islands – is more than 14,500 kilometres (9010 miles) long!

What is a coastal habitat?

A **habitat** is the natural home of a group of **organisms**. Organisms are living things, such as plants and animals. A habitat provides an organism with all that it needs to survive, including food, somewhere safe to shelter and somewhere to have young. The variety and types of plants and animals living on a stretch of coastline habitat depends on the kind of coast that it is.

The British Isles are surrounded by coasts. Some have sandy beaches and others, like this one, have rocky cliffs. ➔

4

Kinds of coastline

There are four main kinds of coastline around the British Isles – rocky, shingle, sandy and muddy. Rocky beaches have cliffs and rocky slopes. Shingle beaches are made up of small stones and are often quite steep. Sandy beaches are made from fine sand. Muddy shores are made up of even smaller bits of rock, which stick together to form mud. Muddy shores usually occur where a river meets the sea. The river washes mud to the coast from further inland. Each bit of coastline is shaped by a number of different things: tides, wind, waves, the kind of rock from which the land is made and whether it is steep, sloping, high or flat.

Interdependent life

The plants and animals on a stretch of coast rely on each other for survival. For example, turnstones are birds that eat sea snails. The sea snails eat seaweed. If there is not enough seaweed growing on a coast, there will be fewer sea snails for turnstones to eat. This reliance on each other is called interdependency.

← Many parts of Britain's coast have different kinds of beach along a single stretch of land. They may have cliffs at the back, with rocks at their base and sand running down to the sea.

How do coasts form?

Coasts are shaped by the power of the sea's waves. As wind blows across the surface of the sea, waves form until they hit land. Small waves gently lap the land, but high waves can crash onto shorelines with tremendous force. Waves shape many of the coastlines in the British Isles by **erosion** – the wearing away of rocks over time. Waves also create beaches by **deposition** – depositing or building up sand and stones along a shore.

How does erosion work?

When waves crash into land, day in and day out, they can slowly wear it away. Strong waves often carry stones or sand with them. These things act like sandpaper to scratch away bits of rock. Some kinds of rock are fairly soft and erode more quickly than others. In these places waves create bays, large curved scoops out of the land where you often find sandy beaches. Waves can also carve caves out of rock. When waves erode rock from the lower part of a cliff, the upper part eventually falls into the sea.

↖ The caves that waves carve out provide shelter for some animals of the sea, such as this grey seal.

What is deposition?

Seabeds are full of bits of gravel, sand and stones. Rivers that flow into the sea bring with them mud and sand from the land. When chunks of eroded rocks fall into the sea, the action of the waves grinds them together and breaks them into smaller and smaller pieces. This creates pebbles and sand. When waves move quickly on to land they carry these bits, which we call **sediment**, with them. As the water flows slowly out again, it leaves some of the sand and pebbles behind. These deposits form beaches.

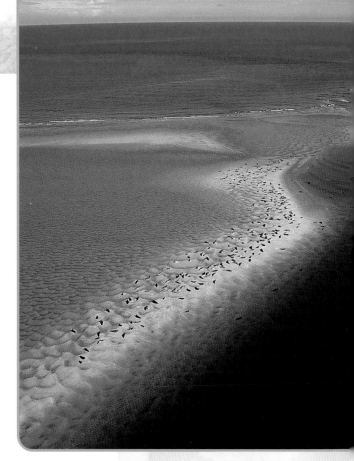

↑ Sometimes the sea piles up a line of sand or gravel out from the land. These ridges are called spits and seals may stop on them to rest.

Limpets

Many coastal animals have ways of coping with the force of waves that could batter or wash them away. Limpets are small animals with tough shells that are cone-shaped so waves flow around them. Limpets grip on to a rock using a muscular foot to avoid being dislodged by waves. Limpets move around when the tide is in to feed on seaweed and tiny **algae** on the rocks.

Changing with the tides

Along every open sea coast in the world the **tide** comes in and goes out twice a day. High tide is when the sea rises up the shore; low tide is when it has flowed out again. The complete explanation for tides is quite complicated. Basically tides happen because of the way the Moon's **gravity** pulls on water in the oceans as the Earth spins round.

Waters of life

Waves crashing on to a shore may look dangerous, but the water that comes in with the tide is the source of life to many coastal creatures. In the sea there are millions of floating plants and animals, most of which are so small you would need a microscope to see them. Together these tiny **organisms** are called **plankton**. When the tide comes in, small animals on the shore eat plankton from the incoming water. These small animals are in turn eaten by larger coastal animals.

A barnacle is a small animal that clings on to rocks. Its shell has two parts that open like doors when the tide is in. Barnacles catch plankton by sifting it from the water with hairy legs that they stick out of their shell. ↘

Living with the tides

Animals and plants that live at the coast have to cope with changing and difficult conditions. When the tide comes in they may be pounded with rough waves. While seawater brings food with it, it is also salty and salt is bad for living things because it can dry them out. Then, when the tide goes out again, they are exposed to the drying sun and harsh winds. In winter, waves can be rougher and the wind and rain may be accompanied by freezing hail and ice.

Coastal food webs

A **food web** is a diagram that shows how food **energy** is passed from plants to animals. Every food web begins with plants. Plants make their own food using energy from sunlight, in a process called **photosynthesis**. Animals eat plants to get energy, or they eat other animals that have eaten plants. The tiny sea plants in plankton are the first link of most food webs in the sea and on the seashore!

← The living things growing on a rocky shore can tell you how high the tide rises. **Algae** grows where tidewater covers it. Yellow **lichen** grows in the splash zone – above the tide line, but where it gets splashed with a little seawater. Marram grass grows above the splash zone.

Rocky coasts

Rocky coastlines may look bare but there are several different kinds of **habitats** where plants can grow. Sea cliffs are steep rocky slopes at the coast. If a cliff rock is soft, it crumbles easily and little can live on it. If the rock is harder, plants can grow there. They grow on ledges or in cracks and many live along the cliff-top. At the water's edge seaweeds grow on the rocks and in rock pools. Rock pools are dips in the rock, which hold water when the **tide** is out.

A cliff-top habitat

Few trees grow on the edge of cliff-tops because there is only a thin layer of soil, and strong winds carry salt from the sea. Only tough plants such as gorse, thistle and heather grow here. Many flowering plants, such as thrift and sea campion, grow low to the ground in rounded cushion shapes. This means their outer leaves protect the rest of the plant from the wind, so they can even grow on the cliff face.

↑ The pink flowers on this cliff-top are thrift and the white ones are sea campion. Spiders, butterflies and other **insects** visit flowering plants like these to feed on the flowers and to lay their eggs on the leaves.

What is seaweed?

Seaweed is a kind of **alga**. Like other plants and algae, seaweeds make their own food using **photosynthesis**. Seaweeds leaves are called fronds and they are flexible, so waves do not break them as they float in the water to reach towards the sunlight. Land plants take in water and other **nutrients** that they need through their **roots**. Seaweeds and other algae absorb all they need straight from the water they live in.

Seaweeds have **holdfasts** to hold them to the surface of rocks. A holdfast may be disc-shaped, or made up of lots of branch-like parts, rather like roots of a land plant. ↓

Kinds of seaweed

Seaweeds can be brown, green or reddish and there are many different shapes. Thong weed looks like long brown leather straps. Bladderwrack has air-filled bladders (bubbles) along its fronds to help them float.

Some seaweeds, such as kelp, live far down the shore, where they are under water most of the time. Others, like bladderwrack, live higher up. Many seaweeds have a coating of slime to stop them drying up when they are out of water at low tide.

Wildlife on rocky coasts

You can find wildlife on all levels of a rocky coast. On the flat tops of cliffs above the shore there may be many different animals such as rabbits, foxes and **insects** among the plants. Only seabirds can land on the cliff face and at its edge. Some come to the ledges of sea cliffs to make their nests. **Predators**, such as foxes, cannot reach them here. However, flying predators such as great black-backed gulls circle around nest sites and snatch eggs and chicks.

Nesting on the cliff face

Some birds, such as guillemots and razorbills, simply lay their eggs on ledges or crannies. Black shags, gannets and cormorants make messy nests out of seaweed and twigs. Their eggs are often blotchy brown so they are **camouflaged** against the rock.

On cliffs that have a deep enough layer of soil, puffins dig burrows to lay their eggs in, or move into old rabbit holes. This puffin parent has caught sand eels from the sea and is bringing them back to feed its young. ➜

Life among the seaweeds

Many animals shelter among seaweeds along the shoreline, especially when the **tide** goes out. Seaweeds keep them moist, shelter them from bad weather and predators, and provide food for some. Periwinkles, a kind of colourful sea snail, grate off small amounts of seaweed to eat with a tongue covered in tiny hooks. Sea slugs and snails also attach their eggs to seaweeds, because it keeps them moist and hidden and stops the eggs from being washed away. You may also see dogfish egg cases lashed to kelp lower down the shore. Some seabirds, such as turnstones, wander amongst the seaweed, searching for sea snails to eat.

Crabs

Crabs are the waste disposal experts of the coast. They eat almost anything they can find. A crab has five pairs of legs that it uses to scuttle sideways. The front legs have strong pincers for picking up food. The crab's shell is called a carapace. A carapace does not grow as a crab does. When most crabs outgrow their carapace they throw it off and hide while the new one beneath stretches and hardens to protect them.

The hermit crab has another tactic – it moves into an empty shell that once belonged to another animal! The crab in this picture is a velvet swimming crab. It is eating a fish that it caught.

Rock pools, Pembrokeshire

The rocky shore of Dale, Pembrokeshire in south-west Wales is covered in rock pools that are rich in plant and animal life. Down by the water's edge, the pools contain some animals that usually live there and some that may have been stranded there when the tide went out.

↑ This map shows the location of Dale and the rocky coast around it. The pale blue areas are water.

Life in the rock pools

Starfish roam the rock pools at Dale to eat sea anemones, mussels and other shellfish, using the tiny mouth in the middle of their body. Most types of starfish have five limbs, which each have hundreds of tiny sucker feet to move them around. Dogwhelks are a type of sea snail that eats barnacles. They twist their sharp tongues between the doors of a barnacle's shell to open it and then they eat the animal inside.

↑ This rock pool is a permanent home to the limpets, different seaweeds and crusty sponges that coat its sides.

Sea anemones

Have you ever seen what look like blobs of dark red jelly in rock pools? These are beadlet anemones, common in the rock pools at Dale. When the tide comes in about 200 fine **tentacles** emerge from their top. The tentacles wave about in water and sting **prey**, such as tiny crabs, shrimps and fish, with poison. Then they push the prey into the mouth in the centre of the anemone's body. After its meal, the anemone spits out any hard parts, like bits of shell!

Shrimps and prawns feed on **plankton** in the water of the Dale rock pools. They are almost transparent (see-through) so that **predators** have trouble spotting them. Grey sea slugs are about 10 centimetres long and they feed on sea anemones in rock pools. Amazingly, a sea slug does not eat an anemone's stinging tentacles, but absorbs them into its back to defend itself!

Rock pool fish

Rock pool fish, such as gobies and blennies, are usually about as long as your little finger. They have a **streamlined** shape that lets the water flow around them, so they can swim more easily. Both are greeny-brown so that they are **camouflaged** against the rock and weed in a pool. Gobies eat shrimps. Blennies have sharp little teeth to crunch barnacles off rocks and to eat dead crabs and other dead animals they find.

Get this!

Both starfish and crabs can grow new limbs if they lose one. If a crab's leg is trapped under a stone it can break it off and grow a new one within weeks!

↑ Oystercatchers use their long orange-red beaks to open cockles, mussels and other sea snails. They find these on rocks and in rock pools at low tide at Dale.

15

Sand and shingle shores

Sand and shingle shores are difficult places for plants to live. At the top of the beach, away from salty seawater and shifting sand and pebbles, some plants can take hold, but life is still tough. There is nothing to shelter living things from the full force of the sun, wind and rain. Also, land plants need fresh water to live, but rainwater quickly drains away through sand and shingle.

Annual plants

Some coastal plants cope with these problems by only growing in the summer when the weather is not so harsh. Such plants, including sea rocket, are called **annuals**. They develop from a **seed**, which spends winter in the ground, then begins to grow the following spring. Annuals flower and then die at the end of summer. The sea rocket plant has small pink flowers. These produce seeds in little pods (cases) that float into the sea. The pods wash up onto a new stretch of shore where they wait until the following spring to grow.

↖ The yellow horned poppy has large golden flowers that produce seeds in pods curved like a cow's horn. As the seed pods dry, they twist and split open to fling the seeds away.

Ways of growing

Many coastal plants grow extra-deep **roots**. The yellow horned poppy has a deep root to anchor it in shifting sand and shingle and to find water. The sea holly's root can reach over a metre long. This plant also has tough holly-like leaves that have a waterproof coating to stop them drying up. To keep out of the path of strong and drying sea breezes, many coastal plants, such as bindweed, keep low to the ground, growing outwards across sand and shingle.

Along the strandline

Most of the plants you might find on a beach are piles of dead, smelly seaweeds! The strandline is the line where high **tides** come farthest up a beach, dropping dead seaweeds, shells, litter and other floating waste from the sea as they retreat. Strandlines are an important source of food for **insects**, such as sandhoppers. They help to break down the rotting tangled seaweeds so that their **nutrients** wash downshore. These tiny pieces help to feed animals under the sand. The strandline also provides insects, such as sandhoppers, with a place to hide as they move along the beach. That is why you often see seabirds patrolling the strandline, looking for **prey** to eat.

Wildlife on sandy shores

For some people, a wide sandy shore looks rather like a dry desert, bare of plants and empty of life. In fact, below the sand there is a busy world full of animals, feeding and hunting.

Down in the sand

There are millions of **molluscs** under the surface of a sandy shore. Most molluscs have two hinged shells. The shells close for safety and to stop them drying out, and open to feed and move. Some molluscs feed on the tiny plants among **plankton**. Cockles have two grooved shells. They push up to the surface with a muscular foot when the **tide** comes in. They stick out two tubes called siphons to feed.

Other molluscs are **predators**; they feed on the flesh of small animals. The common necklace shell is a sea snail that eats two-shelled molluscs like cockles. It bores a neat hole into one shell of the cockle using its tube-like mouth and sucks out the flesh. Some people make necklaces with the holey shells that are left – and that is how the necklace shell got its name.

Razorshells come to the surface when the tide covers them. They strain bits of food out of the water and move swiftly back under the sand when the tide goes out. ↓

Worms of the coast

There are also different kinds of worms beneath the sand. A sandmason is a kind of sea-worm that builds itself a tube to live in out of grains of sand and tiny shell pieces. The worm comes up to the top of its tube to feed when the tide is high, and goes back down into its tube when the tide is low. Ragworms are hunters. They burrow through sand to catch **prey**, such as lugworms, in their jaws. Ragworms are greeny-purple, about 20 centimetres long and as thick as a person's finger. They have teeth that can give you a nasty bite!

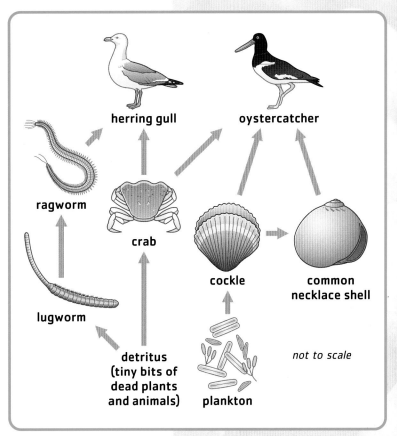

herring gull

oystercatcher

ragworm

crab

cockle

common necklace shell

lugworm

detritus (tiny bits of dead plants and animals)

plankton

not to scale

↑ This is a **food web** for a sandy shore. Many birds, such as oystercatchers and gulls, pull worms and molluscs out of the sand with their beaks.

Lugworms

When walking on a beach you may have seen strange coils of sand below the tide line, like the ones shown here. These are made by large brown lugworms, which live in U-shaped burrows below the surface. This worm feeds by swallowing sand from the burrow entrance and taking tiny bits of detritus (rotted dead plants and animals) from the sand as it passes through its body. The lugworm then passes the sand out of the other end, where it forms the worm-shaped coils on the surface!

Bantham Dunes, Devon

Bantham Beach is a large sandy shore on the south-west coast of Devon. Over many years the wind has blown dry sand up from the beach to the top of the shore. This has formed many small hills called sand dunes. The sand dunes of Bantham are a rich **habitat** for a variety of plants and animals.

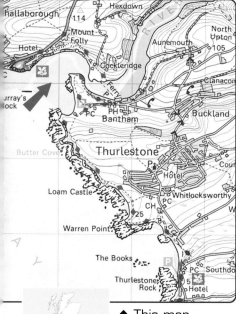

↑ This map shows you where Bantham is. The arrow shows the position of the beach and the dunes behind.

Life among the dunes

Few plants can grow on totally bare, dry sand because the tiny pieces of sand are always moving in the wind. Marram grass has long, spreading **roots** that allow it to take hold. The base of its **stems** trap sand blowing in the wind, and its roots help to bind the sand. That lets sand dunes grow into large mounds. Without marram grass there would only be piles of bare sand moving with the wind. Other plants, such as sea bindweed with its pink and white trumpet-shaped flowers, grow on these mounds. Butterflies, moths and other **insects** come to feed on the **nectar** of flowering plants like these and to lay their eggs on their stems and leaves.

The six-spot burnet moth caterpillar feeds on plants, such as clover and vetch. Its bright colouring helps protect it by warning predators that it tastes bad.➔

Birds in the dunes

Some seabirds make their nests in the upper parts of beaches, as they do at Bantham Dunes. Sand dunes provide shelter from the wind and rain and hold warmth. The long leaves of the marram grass hide nests from **predators** that might try to eat eggs or chicks. Sandwich terns nest at Bantham. They are small seabirds with light grey wings, white throats and black caps. Like many seabirds, they spend most of their time out at sea. They only come to land to **breed**.

Get this!

Small snails feed on broken seashells at Bantham Dunes. These provide an important source of **calcium** for snails. They need it to grow their own shells!

Rabbits

There is a huge network of rabbit burrows in Bantham Dunes. Rabbits often make burrows in sand dunes because the ground is easy to dig and sand dunes are fairly quiet places. Rabbits dig many underground tunnels that together form a network called a warren. They mostly come out in evenings and mornings to eat plants. If it is quiet they feed in the daytime, too. Rabbits make tracks in the sand like the ones here on the right. Look out for them next time you are walking among sand dunes.

Life of the mudflats

Mudflats are muddy coasts that form on **estuaries**. Estuaries are the wide mouths of rivers where they meet the sea. Mudflats are soaked with freshwater for some of the time, then gently flooded with salty sea water when the **tides** come in.

Mudflat plants

The kinds of plants you will see on muddy shores change as you get further inland, just as they do on a rocky shore. By the water's edge, seaweeds cling to rocks. Slightly further up there are plants that can cope with salty water and being covered by the tides. Cordgrass takes in sea water through its **roots** and then disposes of the salt through tiny holes in its leaves. Other plants, such as sea purslane, have fleshy leaves that get fatter as they store freshwater. At the edge of the mud there may be colourful flowering plants, such as sea aster. This plant also has fleshy leaves. It has tall daisy-like flowers to attract bees and other **insects** to **pollinate** its flowers.

Glasswort

Glasswort is one of the few flowering plants that can survive in places where it gets covered by tides. It looks like a small shiny cactus plant. Glasswort takes in freshwater when it rains and stores it in its bright green stems. This stored water stops the glasswort from drying out.

Animal life

Mudflats are a rich **habitat** for small animals. There are even more worms, crabs, shrimps and **molluscs** such as mussels and cockles, living in mud than there are in a similar area of sand. Many feed on the tiny floating plants or animal remains in the water. For example, spire snails trap bits of food on the sticky mucus (slime) they make to slide about on. Many birds nest in the plants at the edge of mudflats and feed on the small animals in the mud. Birds, such as herons, curlews and shelducks, wade through shallow water and mud to catch a meal.

Birds and their beaks

The birds that feed on the mudflats have different beaks, depending on how deep they probe the mud for food. For example, curlews have very long curved beaks to probe deep into mud. Redshanks, with their distinctive red legs, have medium-length beaks to feed in shallower mud. Grey plovers have short beaks and they scurry about picking food from the surface.

Shelducks push their shovel-shaped beaks through the surface of soft mud to sieve out spire snails. ↓

Strangford Lough, in Northern Ireland, is one of the largest sea inlets in the British Isles. An inlet is where a large finger of sea cuts into the land. The **tides** flow in to the Lough through a thin entrance called the Narrows. The lough has about 240 kilometres (150 miles) of coastline, including a massive area of **mudflats**.

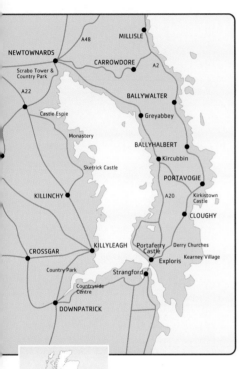

↑ This map shows Strangford Lough. The Narrows are the area at the bottom between Strangford and Portaferry.

Underwater meadows

One of the most important plants in the mudflats here is eelgrass. The long, slender green leaves of this grass-like plant float under the seawater to reach the light and its **roots** anchor it in the mud. Eelgrass flowers are very small and hidden at the bottom of the leaves. The **seeds** they produce float in the water and start to grow in mud elsewhere. The roots of the spreading eelgrass plants hold the mud together. The plants also slow down the water, making a calm and sheltered **habitat** often called an underwater meadow. When eelgrass plants die, they rot down and their **nutrients** feed many different animals under the mud, too.

Strong currents in the Narrows expose dense kelp forests. Kelp is just one of over 2000 species of plants and animals that can be found in the Lough. Of these, 28 are found only here! →

24

Life among the eelgrass

Many animals and other plants live among eelgrass meadows. Tiny plants and **algae** may grow on the leaves and roots. Colourful anemones, worms and sea slugs all shelter and feed among eelgrass. The nutrient-rich grass also attracts some rare birds. Every year, nearly 20,000 light-bellied brent geese fly to Strangford Lough from Canada to feed there over the winter months.

Fish of the meadows

Lots of small fish, such as pipefish, gobies and wrasse, live in the underwater meadows. Other fish lay their eggs here. When the young hatch they can feed in the safety of the beds until they are old enough to swim to sea. There are also two kinds of pipefish that live in the seagrass beds. They feed mainly on small crabs.

Pipefish

Pipefish, as their name suggests, are shaped like thin pipes. They are hard to spot at Strangford Lough because they are browny-green and they swim vertically among the eelgrass plants. Pipefish are related to seahorses. In both animals, it is the male that carries the young in his pouch until they are ready to hatch.

Coasts in danger

The greatest threat to coastal **habitats** and wildlife comes from people. For example, scientists believe that **climate change**, caused by the **polluting** gases that humans are pumping into the atmosphere, is going to make sea levels rise higher up shores and bring far more storms in the future. This means the wave **erosion** that already happens will get much, much worse.

Get this!

When pollution affects one part of a coastal food web, other things are affected, too. When seals eat fish that have fed on polluted plankton, the build-up of chemicals in their bodies make some unable to have young.

Pollution

People pollute the waters around Britain's coast in various ways. When people drop litter and fishermen dump fishing lines or nets this is a kind of pollution that can injure or choke seabirds and other animals. Chemicals from factory waste and farm **pesticides** may run into rivers and then into the sea. In some places, the extra **nutrients** in **sewage** waste that drains into the sea encourages the growth of **algae** weed that chokes other living things in coastal waters.

Oiled birds

Oil spills or leaks from ships at sea also harm coastal wildlife. Sea birds, such as this common scoter, are often killed by oil. Oil clogs the bird's feathers which may cause it to drown or freeze. When a bird tries to clean its feathers it swallows some of the oil, which poisons it.

The trouble with tourism

Many people visit coastlines to walk, picnic and play, but if they do not follow footpaths they can cause erosion. They can wear down land near the edge of a cliff so chunks of rock fall away. Or they may walk on fragile plants and stop them growing. People can also disturb nesting seabirds if they walk too close to them on sand dunes.

Building at the coast

When people build on coasts they change that stretch of shore dramatically. Some people argue that building hotels, piers, golf courses and marinas at coasts brings visitors to the area and work for local people. Others argue that these changes destroy vital plant and animal habitats and may not be good for people in the long run. For example, many coastal **mudflats**, which are precious wildlife habitats, have been drained and filled for farming and building.

When people remove sand from beaches to use for building, they may kill animals in the sand, remove the strandline or affect the coastal habitat in other ways. ↓

Protecting coasts

There are organizations that work to protect the coasts around Britain, but there is also a lot that individuals can do, too.

Seashore code

Whenever you visit the coast it is a great chance to study the wildlife there, but you should always follow these simple rules.

→ Enjoy looking in rock pools, but take care. Watch where you put your feet, turn rocks gently and always put them back where you found them so that you don't destroy animals' homes.

→ If you pick up a limpet or catch a fish in a net, always put them back into the same rock pool. Make sure a shell is empty before you take it home.

→ Never leave litter. Take it home with you or bin it.

→ Avoid disturbing seabirds and their nests, especially those that nest on the ground and among the dunes.

→ Keep to the paths on coastal and cliff walks.

Giant leatherback turtles

Did you know that giant leatherback turtles visit the sea off the south-west coast of England to feed on jellyfish? Sadly, many are dying because they mistake floating plastic bags for their favourite food. Help to stop this by using fewer plastic carriers and disposing of them properly.

↑ These volunteers are helping to clear rubbish off the beach at Weston-Super-Mare, south-west England.

Can people prevent wave erosion?

Longshore drift is the term for water currents that sweep along a coastline close to shore. Longshore drift can **erode** a beach by dragging sand and pebbles sideways along it. Groynes are wooden barriers that slow down longshore drift by trapping sand that the waves move along, to stop it being swept too far along the coast. On some coastlines, people build sea walls to prevent erosion of the shore.

Conservation groups

Conservation means taking action to protect plants and animals and their habitats. Many conservation organizations raise funds from ordinary people to work to protect coasts. Some, such as the National Trust, use the money to buy stretches of coastline and care for them so that no one builds on them or damages them. Other organizations, such as Friends of the Earth, try to educate people about the dangers of **pollution** and other threats to the coastline. They also encourage governments to make more laws to protect the coasts.

Get this!

The National Trust protects one mile of coastline in every five in England, Wales and Northern Ireland.

Some people steal birds' eggs ↗ from nests. Seabirds that nest along this stretch of Norfolk coast are protected by the police.

Glossary

alga/algae organisms that can make their own food by photosynthesis. Many people class algae as plants although they do not have leaves, stems or roots.

annual plant that grows from a seed, flowers, makes seeds and dies all within one season

breed when a male and female animal have babies

calcium chemical that animals need to grow bones and shells

camouflage colours and patterns that help hide an animal's body against its background

climate change various polluting gases trap the Sun's heat around the Earth causing the Earth's climate to get warmer and wetter

deposition when material such as sand is deposited on (added to) an area

energy all living things need energy in order to live and grow

erosion when land is worn away

estuary part of river where fresh river water mixes with salty sea water and the water level changes with the tides

food web diagram that shows the order in which food energy is passed on from plants to animals

gravity force that attracts things towards large bodies such as Moon or Earth

habitat natural place where groups of plants and animals live

holdfast part of seaweed that holds on to rocks

insect small six-legged animals which, when adult, have bodies divided into three sections: head, thorax (chest) and abdomen (stomach)

lichen small, plant-like organism often found on bare rocks. A lichen is a mixture of algae and fungus growing together.

mollusc type of animal, such as snail or octopus

mudflats flat muddy areas along estuaries

nectar sugary substance plants make to attract insects, which like to eat it

nutrients kinds of chemicals found in foods that nourish plants and animals

organism living thing

pesticides chemical sprays farmers and gardeners use to kill insect pests

photosynthesis process by which plants make their own food using water, carbon dioxide (a gas in the air) and energy from sunlight

plankton microscopic organisms that live in the surface waters of the oceans

pollinate when pollen from the male part of a plant combines with an ovule (egg) in the female part to form seeds

pollute/pollution when something harms part of the environment (natural world)

predator animal that catches and eats other animals

prey animal that is caught and eaten by another animal

roots plant parts that anchor plants firmly in the ground and take in water and nutrients

sediment fine particles (tiny pieces) of sand, gravel or mud carried in water

seeds parts of a plant that contain the beginnings of a new plant

sewage human bodily waste carried away from buildings in pipes

stem plant part that holds up the leaves and flower

streamlined shape that is pointed or rounded allowing water or air to flow around it easily

tentacles long, slim finger-like body parts some animals use for feeling or grasping

tide rise and fall of the sea. At high tide the sea rises up the shore. At low tide it flows down again.

Find out more

Books

Collins Pocket Guide to the Sea Shore of Britain and Europe, Peter Hayward, Tony Nelson-Smith and Chris Shields (Harper Collins, 1996)

Taking Action: Friends of the Earth, Louise Spilsbury (Heinemann Library, 2000)

Taking Action: Greenpeace, Louise Spilsbury (Heinemann Library, 2000)

BBC Wildlife publishes a selection of posters showing shells you might find on the beach and rock pool wildlife.

Websites

There is lots of information about how coasts form and how they change at:
www.bbc.co.uk/schools/riversandcoasts
and about coastal habitats at:
www.bbc.co.uk/nature/animals/wildbritain/habitats

The Wildlife Trust website has a section called 'Wildlife Watch' at: www.wildlifetrusts.org

Conservation organizations

To find out what Friends of the Earth is doing to protect Britain's coasts, check out its website at:
www.foe.co.uk
The Marine Conservation Society lists how clean British beaches are and helps conserve coastal wildlife. See:
www.mcsuk.org

The National Trust looks after coasts, countryside and buildings in England and Wales. Its website is:
www.nationaltrust.org.uk
The National Trust for Scotland has a similar role. Its website is: www.nts.org.uk

Index

Titles in the *Wild Habitats of the British Isles* series:

Hardback   0 431 12120 6

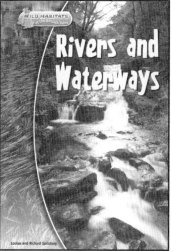

Hardback   0 431 12121 4

Hardback   0 431 12124 9

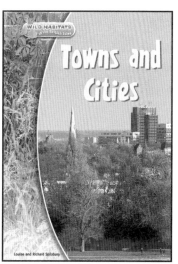

Hardback   0 431 12123 0

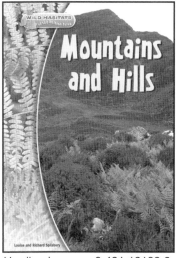

Hardback   0 431 12122 2

Hardback   0 431 12125 7

Find out about the other Heinemann Library titles on our website www.heinemann.co.uk/library